Science

Brian Williams

Heinemann Library
Chicago, Illinois

© 2002 Reed Educational and Professional Publishing
Published by Heinemann Library,
an imprint of Reed Educational & Professional Publishing,
Chicago, Illinois

Customer Service 888-454-2279
Visit our website at www.heinemannlibrary.com.

Designed by Tinstar Design
Originated by Ambassador Litho
Printed by Wing King Tong in Hong Kong/China

06 05 04 03 02
10 9 8 7 6 5 4 3 2 1

Library of Congress Cataloging-in-Publication Data
Williams, Brian, 1959-
  Science / Brian Williams.
      p. cm. -- (Great inventions)
Includes bibliographical references and index.
  ISBN 1-58810-214-9
  1. Inventions--History--Juvenile literaure. 2.
Inventors--History--Juvenile literaure. [1. Inventions--History. 2.
Inventors--History.] I. Title. II. Series.
  T15 .W688 2001
  609--dc21
                              2001000108

Acknowledgments
The author and publishers are grateful to the following for permission to reproduce copyright material:
Cover photographs: Mary Evans, Photodisc, and Science Photo Library.
pp. 5, 9, 14, 18, 19, 21, 24, 31, 34, 36, 38 Science and Society Picture Library; p. 6 Royal Ontario Museum/ Corbis; p. 7 Chris Rushton; pp. 8, 12, 22, 28 Hulton Getty; p. 10 Bettmann/Corbis; p. 11 Deep Light Prod/Science Photo Library; p. 16 Ann Ronan Picture Library; p. 20 Owen Franken/Corbis; p. 23 K. Flemming/Corbis; p. 26 Photodisc; p. 29 Jerry Walker/Science Photo Library; pp. 30, 41 Layne Kennedy/Corbis; p. 32 FPG; p. 40 Culture Archive; p. 42 J. Mason/Science Photo Library; p. 43 National Air and Space Museum, Smithsonian Institute.

Every effort has been made to contact copyright holders of any material reproduced in this book. Any omissions will be rectified in subsequent printings if notice is given to the publisher.

Some words are shown in bold, **like this.** You can find out what they mean by looking in the glossary.

A note about dates: in this book, dates are followed by the letters B.C.E. (Before the Common Era) or C.E. (Common Era). This is instead of using the older abbreviations B.C. (Before Christ) and A.D. (*Anno Domini*, meaning "in the year of our Lord"). The date numbers are the same in both systems.

Contents

Introduction

Science means knowledge. Scientists gather knowledge by studying facts and through experiments—observing and recording what they see and can measure. Today, most scientific research is done by large teams of scientists. In the past, scientists usually worked alone and did experiments with **apparatus** they made themselves. They received little encouragement. Scientists often faced hostility, and some were even accused of practicing black magic.

Science began thousands of years ago when people looked at the sun and stars, animals and plants, mountains and rivers, and tried to figure out laws to explain what they saw. Scientists provided solutions to practical, everyday problems, like inventing machines to raise water from a river to irrigate fields. They also investigated the unknown. The Ancient Greeks were probably the first people to take what they could see as a starting point, rather than what people had always believed. They were "science detectives" and made important discoveries, even though Greek scientists rarely took science from ideas to actual inventions, making something never seen before.

After the Greeks, there was little real scientific detective work for 1,000 years. Old ideas went unchallenged and new ideas spread very slowly in a world with few roads and even fewer books. The Chinese invented gunpowder some time between 600 and 900 C.E. but did their best to keep it a secret. It was not until the 1200s that people in Europe learned of this amazing new invention.

All this started to change in the 1600s, when "modern" science really began. Old ideas were reexamined by scientists using new scientific instruments, such as the thermometer. By using facts, scientists came up with laws to explain why a balloon gets bigger when you blow it up, why apples fall downward, and why the lid of a pot rattles when the water inside it boils.

In the 1700s, there arose a new belief in progress, the belief that science and invention could solve any problem and would, in time, bring about a better world. The **Industrial Revolution** began in the 1700s with more inventions than at any time in history, including factory and farm machines that changed people's lives. These machines were driven by new sources of energy—first steam, then gas, and later electricity and gasoline engines.

Modern science grew from medieval alchemy, a mixture of science and magic. Early scientists hoped to discover the secret of eternal life.

This book looks at some of those inventions that made our modern world, from gunpowder to nuclear power. Some of their inventors were famous scientists. Others are fading names in old books or people whose names are not known. Without their inventions, some made after years of patient research and others by chance, we would not be living in the fast-changing, high-tech world of today.

Porcelain, 850

The Romans ate off pottery plates, but in the Middle Ages most people dined from wooden or metal dishes, or put their food on hunks of bread. "China" tableware made from porcelain was not produced outside China until the 1500s, and it was not perfected in Europe until 1707.

Pottery is a kind of **ceramic,** like glass or brick. It is made from clay. Everyday pottery, or earthenware, was first dried hard in the sun and later baked in an oven called a kiln. Potters were among the first technologists, turning a soft and easily shaped material—clay—into a hard, watertight, and useful object.

Chinese porcelain, like these vases made in the 1600s, was so fine that people in the West were eager to make porcelain themselves. However, the technology was tricky, and they did not perfect it until much later.

Fine china

The Chinese were experts at making pottery. In 850, Chinese potters figured out how to make a new and beautiful kind of pottery. They mixed a kind of clay called kaolin with a mineral called petuntse, or feldspar. They molded the soft mixture into shape and then baked it at a high temperature, around 2500 °F (1,400 °C). The kaolin and petuntse fused to make a glass-like pottery so hard that a knife could chip it, but not cut it.

This was the first true porcelain. It could be decorated and glazed with a mixture of powdered glass and minerals. When the porcelain was put back into the kiln, the heat melted the glaze into the clay. The Chinese emperors' love of porcelain jars, dishes, and plates kept the porcelain workers busy.

In the 1200s, the Italian traveler Marco Polo spent seventeen years in China. When he returned to Italy in 1295, one of the wonders he described was porcelain. A few pieces were sold to rich Western rulers, but how to make porcelain remained a Chinese secret.

Europeans make porcelain

In the 1570s, potters in Florence, Italy, managed to make "soft-paste" porcelain. It could be cut, unlike Chinese porcelain. Often nine out of ten pieces came out of the kiln incorrectly and had to be thrown away. French potters also invented a soft-paste porcelain, in 1675, and it was named after the royal factory at Sèvres near Paris.

The Wedgwood factory in Staffordshire, England, began making porcelain in 1800. This photo shows pieces being put into a modern kiln for firing.

Around 1707, German chemist Johann Böttger, in partnership with the potter Ehrenfried von Tschirnhaus, discovered at last how to make porcelain that was hard and "true," like Chinese. The German factory of Meissen became the leader in European porcelain-making. In 1800, the British pottery companies of Spode and Wedgwood added bone ash to clay, making "bone china," which was better for everyday use because it was less likely to chip than pure porcelain.

Porcelain Teeth

An unexpected use for porcelain was for making false teeth. First tried in 1770, this was very successful because porcelain teeth looked whiter than the false teeth used before. Most people did without when their teeth fell out or were removed, and some people had suffered the embarrassment of wearing wooden dentures or teeth taken from dead people.

1200 B.C.E.	850 C.E.	1530s	1575	1710	1800
Chinese potters use the wheel to shape clay pots.	The Chinese begin making porcelain.	Pottery plates become fashionable in Europe.	Italian potters make "soft-paste" porcelain.	The Meissen factory starts making porcelain ware in Germany.	Spode and Wedgewood factories begin making "bone china."

Gunpowder, 900

Some time around 900, a Chinese inventor created gunpowder. He was an **alchemist,** mixing together "magical medicines" that he hoped would prolong life and cure all diseases. By accidentally mixing saltpeter (potassium nitrate), sulfur, and charcoal (carbon), this unknown inventor produced a black powder that exploded violently when touched by a flame.

Fireworks and black magic

The Chinese enjoyed the bangs and sparks of this amazing powder and used it to make fireworks. They experimented with stuffing powder into a tube so that the explosive energy was released in one direction. They put gunpowder into the first rockets, which they fired as weapons and to light up the sky in firework displays.

News of this remarkable powder spread slowly across Asia and into Europe. Arab scientists studied it and **Crusaders** heard about it. In about 1260, an English **friar** named Roger Bacon read an Arab scientist's description of gunpowder and its ingredients. He made some himself, to the alarm of the Catholic Church, which regarded such science as evil magic.

The German monk-alchemist Berthold Schwarz may have made the first gunpowder in Europe, and the first cannon.

The first cannon

A German monk, Berthold Schwarz, is said to have made the first gun, about 1313. He packed gunpowder into a metal tube that was closed at one end, pushed in a round stone, and set off the gunpowder with a lighted match. The explosion sent the stone flying out of the mouth of the tube. For 300 years, stone castles had withstood warfare but from then on, no stone wall was safe against guns. Armies were quick to try this new weapon, and guns were being fired on the battlefield by the 1320s.

The first guns fired giant arrows or stones, until metal balls proved to be better. Early cannons were inaccurate and often blew up, killing or injuring their operators. Clouds of smoke enveloped the battlefield, as the booming guns struck fear into soldiers and blasted holes in castle walls.

The gunpowder age

Gunpowder-making became an industry. In powdermills, workers operating spring-loaded beams pounded the **chemicals** in troughs. An expert "firemaster" made sure that the ingredients were mixed in the correct proportions. Gun makers made stronger gun barrels, and by the 1500s cannons were the main weapons for both land and sea battles. Gunpowder reigned supreme until the 1800s, when more powerful (and less smoky) explosives such as nitroglycerine and dynamite were developed.

The alchemists

Alchemists hoped to find the "Philosopher's Stone," a magical super-**element** that would turn ordinary metals, such as lead, into gold. Many alchemists were tricksters. Some were more like magicians, and others carried out scientific experiments. Alchemy was based on some wrong ideas. By the 1600s, scientists knew that there was no Philosopher's Stone. However, the alchemists did make useful discoveries. They were the first chemists, and some of the equipment they used can still be found in modern laboratories.

The Chinese tried using gunpowder to fire arrows in bunches, although this curious weapon looks as if it would be more dangerous to the soldier holding it while the gunpowder explodes! The first cannons fired giant darts, one dart at a time.

900	1200s	1326	1346	1400s	1866
The Chinese discover how to make gunpowder.	News of gunpowder passes from the Arab world to Europe.	First picture of a cannon in a European book.	Cannons are fired at the Battle of Crecy between the English and French armies.	Gunpowder is used for blasting rocks in mines and quarries.	Alfred Nobel of Sweden invents a new explosive, dynamite.

9

Magnifying Lens, 1200

Before 1000, no one wore eyeglasses, or spectacles. People with failing sight had to do the best they could. Until the 1500s, no scientist had ever looked through a microscope or a telescope. None of these inventions were possible without **lenses.**

How glass was first made

Modern eyeglass lenses are usually made of tough plastic. In the ancient world, glass was the only material through which light could pass easily. The Phoenicians and Egyptians made glass more than 3,000 years ago. An old story tells how some Phoenician sailors lit a fire on a sandy beach and rested their cooking pots on blocks of saltpeter. The heat from the fire fused the silica in the sand with the saltpeter to make glass. People in Syria discovered how to blow glass into different shapes by about 100 B.C.E.

Early spectacles were worn wedged on the nose, or held in the hand on a stalk-like holder. Cheap glasses in metal frames went on sale in the 1800s.

Glass was very expensive. Few houses had glass windows, and only wealthy people drank from glass goblets. Metal was cheaper. The Ancient Greeks used glass flasks filled with water as "burning glasses," to focus the rays of the sun to light a fire.

The mysterious lens

Some time before 1200, an unknown inventor in China or Europe made a magnifying glass, a curved lens that made things look bigger. No scientist yet understood what light was, but something odd happened when a curved piece of glass was held up to the sunlight. Not only did it produce a concentrated area of heat, but it also changed the way things looked. Perhaps a glassmaker polished a piece of leftover glass and made the first lens by accident.

In 1280, an Italian, possibly an inventor named Salvino degli Armati, fitted two lenses together and made what we now call "eyeglasses." The word lens comes from the Latin word for *lentil*, because the first lenses were the same shape as the lentil seed.

People wear crystal glasses

The first glasses, known as "discs for the eyes," were not made of glass. They were made of crystals of a mineral called beryl, set into frames made from wood or animal bone. Beryl was not as clear as glass, but it was tougher and easier to shape and polish. The first eyeglasses had **convex** lenses, to help farsighted people. **Concave** lenses, for nearsighted people, were invented in the 1400s.

New and improved lenses

Oddly, it took scientists 200 years to put lenses together in line, not side by side, to invent the telescope and the microscope. By the 1500s, glassmakers were able to cut and grind lenses much more accurately. Eyeglasses could now be made with glass lenses, and the magnifying glass became a useful scientific tool for studying nature. Without the magnifying lens, outer space and the inner world of the **cell** would have remained unseen mysteries.

The lens became a scientific instrument with the invention of the compound microscope in 1580. Ninety years later, in 1670, Dutch scientist Antoni van Leeuwenhoek made the first scientific observation of microscopic life.

1100s	1268	1451	1590	1608	1887
The Chinese discover the magnifying power of a lens and use lenses to help them read.	In England, Roger Bacon describes how a magnifying glass works and is suspected of practicing magic.	In Italy, the public can buy eyeglasses.	The first microscope is made by Zacharias Jansen.	The telescope is invented.	Glass contact lenses are invented.

Thermometer, 1592

Greek scientists 2,000 years ago did their experiments without any measurements other than "hot" or "cold." There was no way to measure temperature until the invention of the thermometer by the Italian scientist Galileo Galilei in 1592.

The first thermometers

Galileo's thermometer or "thermoscope" was a glass bulb with a long neck. Full of air, it was placed upside down in a dish of spirit of wine, a kind of alcohol. Galileo watched as the water rose part of the way up the neck and then stopped. On a hot afternoon, the level sank as the warm air expanded, but it rose in the cool of the evening, as the air above it contracted.

In about 1612, an Italian doctor, Professor Sanctorius, invented the doctor's thermometer when he put a small thermoscope into the mouth of a feverish patient. Sanctorius also had the idea of adding a scale. He marked the glass tube with 110 marks, from cold (melting snow) to hot (candle heat). In France, Jean Rey, another doctor, made a thermometer filled with water. Other inventors tried using **mercury.** This worked much better.

A thermometer is now part of every doctor's medical bag. This doctor is checking students during a school physical early in the twentieth century.

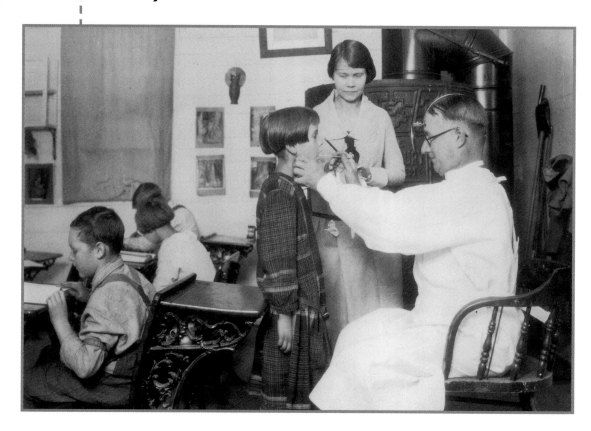

How a doctor's thermometer works

A doctor's thermometer works because the mercury inside the bulb at the bottom expands when it warms up. The mercury is forced out of the bulb and up inside the narrow tube. A notch in the tube just above the bulb stops the mercury from sinking back too quickly. This gives the doctor time to read the scale marked on the side of the thermometer.

Non-liquid thermometers

Some thermometers have no liquid at all. For example, the **bimetallic strip** thermometer in ovens makes use of the difference in expansion of two metals, brass and steel. A strip of brass and a strip of steel are fixed together and bent into a coil fixed at one end. Because brass expands faster than steel when it is heated, the coil is forced to curl and moves a pointer on a dial to show the temperature.

Scales

The early scientists who made thermometers devised their own scales. By 1700, there were over 35 scales! This made it impossible for scientists to compare data. Two scales finally emerged. One was invented in 1714 by Daniel Fahrenheit, using the symbol °F. On this scale, 32° is the melting point of ice and 96° is body temperature (it is actually 98.6°F). Water boils at 212°.

The other is the Celsius or centigrade scale, invented by Swedish astronomer Anders Celsius in 1742. It is used in science and where the metric measuring system is used. It uses 0° for the melting point of ice and 100° for the boiling point of water. Originally, Celsius had it the other way around. 100 was freezing and 0 was boiling! The symbol °C is used for Celsius temperatures.

Galileo the experimenter

Galileo Galilei, who made many experiments with thermometers, discovered that science could get him into trouble. His scientific curiosity and experiments angered the Catholic Church so much that he spent the last eight years of his life under house arrest. In spite of this opposition, Galileo inspired other scientists to experiment. Instruments such as the telescope, thermometer, and barometer were essential tools for the new science.

1592	1714	1730s	1742	1867	1848
Galileo Galilei makes the first working thermometer or thermoscope.	Daniel Farenheit invents his temperature scale.	Clockmaker John Harrison invents the bimetallic strip.	Anders Celsius invents the Celsius or centigrade temperature scale.	In Britain, Thomas Allbutt invents the modern doctor's thermometer.	William Thomson, Lord Kelvin, invents a new temperature scale, later named after him.

Barometer, 1643

The barometer is an instrument for measuring air pressure. It was invented in 1643 by an Italian, Evangelista Torricelli. Important for the study of air and **vacuums,** the barometer also made possible scientific weather forecasting.

Torricelli and his tube

Torricelli was a doctor who had been taught by Galileo Galilei, inventor of the thermometer. Galileo had explained his belief that air has weight and that there must be a weight of air pressing down upon our bodies. How could this pressure be shown to exist?

Torricelli decided to try using a glass tube filled with **mercury,** similar to Galileo's thermometer. He held his finger over the open end and turned over the tube in a bowl containing more mercury. When he removed his finger, he saw the liquid mercury fall inside the tube and stop 30 inches (76 centimeters) above the surface, leaving a space above. Torricelli guessed that the pressure of the air in the atmosphere was pushing down on the surface of the mercury in the bowl and holding the mercury at this level in the tube.

Torricelli kept careful notes of how the tube looked from day to day. On sunny days, the mercury rose higher. On cloudy, windy days it sank. This suggested that air pressure was not the same every day. Perhaps it was the cause of changes in the weather? High pressure meant a fine, calm day. A fall in pressure meant wind and perhaps rain.

The higher you go, the lower it gets

French scientist Blaise Pascal made a barometer filled with water and red wine. Because this liquid was less **dense** than mercury, his first tube had to be 46 feet (14 meters) long to work! Pascal sent his brother-in-law Florin Périer to climb a mountain with a smaller barometer to see what would happen. It showed a fall in pressure going up, but a rise in pressure as the weary climber came down. Pascal reasoned that the higher you went, the lower the air pressure became. You could therefore use the barometer to measure how high you were.

Aneroid barometers

The barometers most often seen in houses today are of the aneroid or non-liquid kind. Inside them is a vacuum chamber. As pressure outside rises, the chamber is compressed inward. The opposite happens when outside pressure falls. This in-and-out movement is transferred through levers and wheels to a needle, which points to figures on a dial.

Blaise Pascal (1623–62)

Pascal was a child **prodigy** who amazed adult mathematicians with his remarkable ability. His sister Jacqueline was equally talented as a writer. Pascal is famous for inventing a calculating machine, but he was also interested in experiments to test the ideas of other scientists, such as Torricelli and Galileo. He became deeply religious after 1654 and spent his last years writing about Christianity.

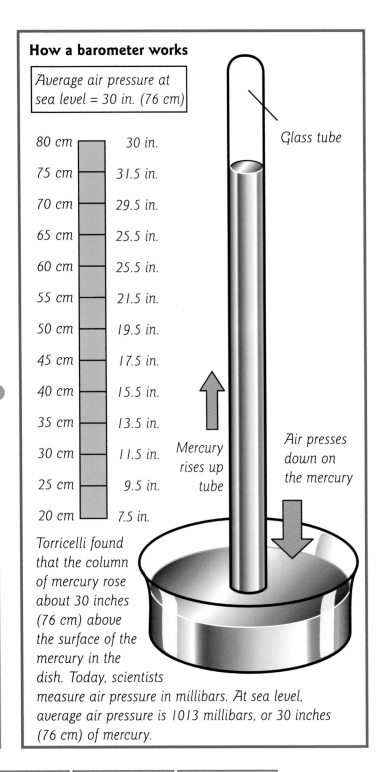

How a barometer works

Average air pressure at sea level = 30 in. (76 cm)

80 cm	30 in.
75 cm	31.5 in.
70 cm	29.5 in.
65 cm	25.5 in.
60 cm	25.5 in.
55 cm	21.5 in.
50 cm	19.5 in.
45 cm	17.5 in.
40 cm	15.5 in.
35 cm	13.5 in.
30 cm	11.5 in.
25 cm	9.5 in.
20 cm	7.5 in.

Glass tube

Mercury rises up tube

Air presses down on the mercury

Torricelli found that the column of mercury rose about 30 inches (76 cm) above the surface of the mercury in the dish. Today, scientists measure air pressure in millibars. At sea level, average air pressure is 1013 millibars, or 30 inches (76 cm) of mercury.

300s B.C.E.	1643 C.E.	1800	1862	1953
Theophrastus, a student of Aristotle, records the first scientific study of weather.	In Italy, Torricelli makes the first mercury-filled barometer.	J. B. Lamarck of France organizes the first international system for observing weather.	James Glaisher and Henry Coxwell climb over 32,800 feet (10,000 meters) in a balloon to study the atmosphere.	The world meteorological organization adopts millibar as the standard unit of atmospheric pressure.

Air Pump, 1650

When the **mercury** in a thermometer drops, it leaves a space above it—a **vacuum.** Creating a perfect vacuum any other way was difficult in the 1600s, without an air pump. The air pump opened up new lines of scientific inquiry.

Air power

Otto von Guericke, a German military engineer, wanted to find out how air behaved. About the same time that Torricelli invented the barometer, he designed one of his own, but it was too long to be practical. The barometer proved that air had weight and took up space. It also showed that a vacuum was possible. Von Guericke thought it should be possible to make a pump that would suck air out of a space and create a vacuum.

People watched in astonishment as two teams of horses failed to pull apart Von Guericke's copper bowls. They did not realize how much pressure the air was exerting, even on their own bodies.

The copper bowl test

Von Guericke made his air pump in 1650. To make sure it was airtight, every joint had to be carefully sealed. When he pumped air out of a thin metal container, he was amazed by what happened—the container was crushed by the pressure of the air all around it. In 1654, he performed a spectacular demonstration of air power. Among the audience was the Holy Roman Emperor himself, the ruler of the small states that then made up Germany.

Von Guericke had made two copper bowls, which fitted together to make a sphere. He pumped air out from inside the sphere. Then he challenged his audience to pull the two halves apart. It looked simple, but even with two teams of horses tugging with all their might, the halves stayed firmly together, held in place by the enormous pressure of the air on the outside of the almost airless sphere.

A useful tool

Von Guericke went on to show that sound does not travel through a vacuum and that animals cannot live without air. The air pump became a useful tool for scientists, helping them to show that air is a mixture of gases and to isolate and name the various gases. They figured out the laws that explain the connections between air pressure, volume, and temperature. By sucking air out of a container, scientists could make a vacuum. This led to the invention of the vacuum bottle and the air lock, used by astronauts when leaving and reentering a spacecraft.

Sorry, Aristotle

Aristotle, the most famous scientist of the ancient world, scoffed at the idea of a vacuum. He believed that no such thing could exist. For 2,000 years, scientists who followed Aristotle's teachings declared that "Nature abhors [cannot tolerate] a vacuum." Von Guericke's air pump helped prove the great Greek was wrong.

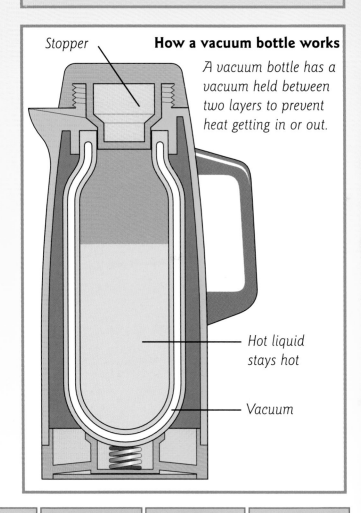

Stopper

How a vacuum bottle works

A vacuum bottle has a vacuum held between two layers to prevent heat getting in or out.

Hot liquid stays hot

Vacuum

200s	1654	1661	1830	1892	1965
Ctesibius invents the bicycle-style pump for pumping water up through a **cylinder.**	Otto von Guericke startles everyone with his vacuum globe trial of strength.	Robert Boyle identifies the laws that explain how the volume and pressure of gases are related.	Thomas Cochrane develops the first air lock, used by divers doing engineering projects.	Sir James Dewar invents the vacuum bottle.	The first astronaut to use an air lock, Alexi Leonov of the former Soviet Union, makes the first space walk.

Steam Engine, 1712

What makes a boiling pot's lid rattle up and down? Many scientists must have watched this and wondered how this power could be used. The Ancient Greeks played with steam toys. In about 60 C.E., Hero of Alexandria made a small **turbine** with steam jets that whizzed around and around on a stand.

Putting steam to work

No one tried to put steam to work until the 1600s, after Otto von Guericke demonstrated how much force air could exert. His air pump inspired other inventors to think about air and steam.

In 1679 Denis Papin, a Frenchman working in London with the scientist and gas expert Robert Boyle, built the world's first pressure cooker. He used steam trapped inside a metal container to cook beef bones until they were soft.

Scottish inventor James Watt learned about machines in his father's workshop. He turned the steam engine from a pump into the powerhouse of industry.

Thomas Savery built a simple steam pump in 1698. The first practical steam engine, however, was built in 1712 by another British inventor, Thomas Newcomen. Newcomen had borrowed an idea from Papin. His engine had a **piston** and a **cylinder.** First, hot steam pushed the piston upward inside the cylinder. Then, cold water was squirted onto the cylinder to **condense** the steam inside. This reduced the pressure in the cylinder, with the result that the air pressure outside pushed the piston downward.

Newcomen's steam engines had a simple "push-and-pull" action and pumped water from deep mines for 50 years or more. They burned a lot of coal or wood and wasted most of the power they produced.

This steam driven hammer, designed by James Nasmyth in 1842, was used to pound iron and steel into shape to make paddle wheels for steamships.

The engine revolution

In 1764, James Watt was given a creaking, wheezing Newcomen engine to repair. He saw how to improve the machine by using the hot steam more efficiently and controlling it with **valves.** Watt turned the steam pump into an engine for driving any kind of machine. By 1781, he had designed a steam engine with a rotary action. His new engine could be linked by belts or chains to drive factory machines, **weaving** looms, heavy tools, and printing presses.

Other inventors, such as Oliver Evans in the United States and Richard Trevithick in Britain, invented high pressure steam engines, the kind used in the first railroad locomotives. By the 1820s, the world was changing to steam power.

James Watt (1736–1819)

Watt was born in Greenock, Scotland. He went to London when he was nineteen to learn instrument-making. After a year he came home and got a job at Glasgow University. There he made friends with the scientist Joseph Black, an expert in steam and heat. They discussed how to make a better steam engine, and Watt made one. Watt's partnership with businessman Matthew Boulton made him rich enough to spend his last years tinkering in "mechanical pursuits."

1698	1712	1769	1781	1802	1804
Englishman Thomas Savery builds the first working steam pump.	Thomas Newcomen designs a practical steam engine in England.	In France, Nicholas-Joseph Cugnot builds a steam carriage that frightens everyone and is abandoned!	James Watt improves the steam engine.	Oliver Evans builds a high pressure steam engine.	Richard Trevithick builds the first successful steam carriage.

Chronometer, 1759

A chronometer is a ship's timekeeper. The first sea clock that kept accurate time through storms, ice, or tropical heat saved the lives of many sailors. Its inventor was an English carpenter turned clockmaker named John Harrison.

A pendulum clock like this old long-case clock would not keep time at sea. Ships needed a more reliable timekeeper.

The longitude problem

In order to know how far and in what direction a ship has sailed, it is necessary to know what time it is. When Columbus sailed from Spain for the New World in 1492, he relied on the sun to tell the time. Sailers used simple instruments to determine how high the sun appeared above the horizon so they could figure out where they were.

Lines of **latitude** and **longitude** had been marked on maps since 300 B.C.E., but since maps were not accurate, many ships got lost and were never seen again. A sailor could find latitude by taking sun sightings. Longitude was much more tricky, because the sun was no help. Longitude can be found only by comparing the time on board a ship with the time at the home port or some other place of known longitude. Unfortunately, no clock made before 1700 would keep time at sea, because a ship's movement and temperature changes upset the swing of a clock's pendulum.

The answer might be in the stars

Astronomers thought star charts could solve the problem. They showed the apparent changes in the position of stars. However, sailors were not astronomers, and to do the complicated calculations to use star charts took time and skill. At sea, a navigator might have only a momentary glimpse of the stars through storm clouds. In 1714, the British government offered a prize of £20,000, a huge sum, to the first inventor who could solve the longitude problem.

Mr. Harrison's four clocks

John Harrison, from the north of England, traveled to London to bid for the prize. He spent the next 35 years on the project, making three large clocks known as H1, H2, and H3. He built complicated balance systems, weights, ribbons, and springs to make the clocks keep time even in a storm at sea. For H3 he invented the **bimetallic strip** so the pendulum would swing true. He also fitted **bearings,** similar to modern ball bearings.

Harrison then made H4, which looked like a pocket watch. It was tested in 1761 and 1764 on voyages to the West Indies by Harrison's son William. The watch kept nearly perfect time. The British naval board grudgingly awarded Harrison the prize, although he did not receive the full amount until three years before he died in 1776, at the age of 83.

Harrison's "sea clock" and the sextant, invented in 1757, are still trusted today by many sailors, even after the introduction of **satellite**-based navigation systems in the 1990s.

John Harrison's first sea clock, H1, was a complicated and heavy brass machine with four dials showing days of the month, hours, minutes, and seconds. It is still running at the National Maritime Museum in Greenwich, England.

The patient clockmaker

John Harrison was born in 1693, the son of a carpenter. He taught himself science by copying a textbook of lectures lent to him by a local minister. He also taught himself to make clocks. Being familiar with woodwork, he used wood, not metal, for most of the moving parts. A tower clock he made in 1722 for Brocklesby Park in England is still running.

About 1510	1657	1735	1759	1884	1995
Peter Heinlein, in Germany, makes the first spring-powered clock.	Christiaan Huygens of Denmark invents the pendulum clock.	In England, John Harrison completes his first chronometer.	John Harrison builds his H4 watch.	Greenwich Mean Time (GMT) becomes the international standard time.	U.S. Navstar Navigation system can pinpoint a ship's location using satellite data.

Cotton Gin, 1793

The man who did most to expand the cotton industry in the United States was Eli Whitney. He invented a labor-saving machine that made cotton growers more prosperous and helped make the United States the world's leading cotton producer.

The textile industry grows

Cotton has been grown for more than 5,000 years. The cotton plant's fibers provide raw material for the **textile** industry. Before 1700, spinners spun cotton thread and weavers wove it into cloth in their homes. Then they sold the cloth to merchants. In the 1700s, inventors made the first textile machines, which sped up the process to meet the rising demand for cotton textiles.

First, **weaving** was made faster by machine. The new weaving machines were hungry for more cotton yarn, or thread. **Spinning** machines were invented to meet this demand, turning the raw cotton fibers into yarn. The spinners caught up with the weavers.

Slaves worked in the cotton fields of the United States. It was hard work, and so was separating the fibers from the seeds, the task taken over by Whitney's cotton gin.

Cotton picking

Where did cotton start from? In the cotton fields, people still picked the fluffy white seed pods, or bolls, by hand. The fibers had to be separated from the seeds by hand. It was slow and tedious work, and every cotton farm, or plantation, needed hundreds of workers, usually **slaves.**

The colonists began to grow cotton in the 1600s, selling it to British mills. When the United States became independent in 1783, the Americans wanted to expand their cotton industry and make it more profitable. In 1793, Eli Whitney of Georgia invented a new machine to speed up the work in the cotton fields.

Simple roller engines, called "gins," had been tried before, but they were no good for processing the best cotton, called "short staple." It could take a day to sort one pound (half a kilogram) of cotton. Whitney's gin had a handle that turned a **cylinder** full of wire hooks. The hooks pulled the fibers through a mesh, leaving the seeds behind. Then a roller pushed the fibers into a box. One Whitney gin could produce more cotton in a day than 50 people!

Whitney's gin was a rugged machine that plantation workers could use easily and repair if necessary. One machine could do the work of up to fifty people.

Eli Whitney (1765–1825)
Whitney was an amateur mechanic studying law. One evening at the home of his landlady, Catherine Littlefield Greene, he listened to cotton planters at dinner complain of how long it took to sort cotton by hand. Mrs. Greene cheerfully told her guests that smart Mr. Whitney would solve the problem. It took him six months, and Mrs. Greene helped with advice. Unfortunately, she also told the neighbors, and rivals began selling copies of Whitney's gin. He spent years arguing his case in court. He later turned to making guns for the government.

1733	1764	1790s	1793	1796	1940s
John Kay invents the flying shuttle, which speeds up weaving.	James Hargrave's spinning jenny speeds up spinning.	The first cotton mills in the United States start making textiles.	Eli Whitney's cotton gin does the work of 50 people on plantations.	Hogden Holmes improves Whitney's gin by adding saw teeth instead of hooks.	The first machines to pick and strip cotton gradually replace workers.

Safety Matches, 1827

Imagine trying to light a fire without matches. That problem faced everyone from prehistoric times until the 1830s. Matches did not exist. At home, most people tried to keep a fire lit, night and day.

Making fire required effort and patience. Rubbing sticks together to create heat through **friction** was one method. Before 1800, the word "match" meant either a slow–burning fuse of twisted cord, used to set off explosives and guns, or a small sliver of wood dipped in **inflammable** material such as tar or sulfur. This was lit from a fire and used to carry a flame to candles or lamps.

The chemical match

The growing interest in chemistry in the early 1800s led inventors to experiment with a match that would light when its **chemical** tip was rubbed. An early match called the "Lucifer," made in London by Samuel Jones, was a small glass bulb filled with **acid** and coated with other chemicals. To light it, you snapped off the end with a pair of pliers or your teeth. Breaking the glass mixed the acid and chemicals, which set fire to the paper wrapping.

Early matches were known as Lucifers. "Lucifer" means "light-bearing" in Latin. Packed into cheap boxes, matches were easy to carry around.

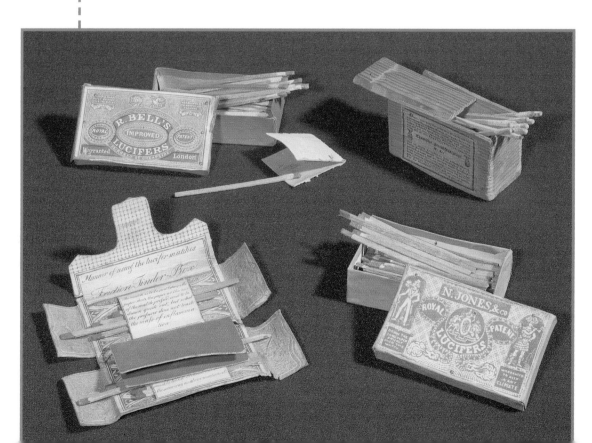

24

The first attempts at matches were unsafe and unreliable. The chemicals were usually poisonous, and the matches either wouldn't light or exploded in a shower of sparks. The first friction matches were made by the English chemist John Walker in 1827. They were slivers of wood or cardboard, tipped with a paste of potassium chloride and antimony sulfide. The matches lit when rubbed between folded sandpaper.

The matchbox man

John Walker was born in northeast England around 1780. He ran a pharmacy. In his spare time he experimented with "lighting mixtures" to make matches. Walker sold his matches in boxes of 50 for 1 shilling (about 5 cents), and each box came with a sheet of folded sandpaper. Although he never **patented** his new match, thinking it an unimportant invention, he sold enough matches to retire and lived comfortably until his death in 1859.

Match making hazards

In 1831, French inventor Charles Sauria made the first white phosphorus matches. These flared up every time and had less of a bad smell than Walker's matches. People were eager for the new matches, and the first match factory was set up in Vienna in 1833.

Match making was dangerous work because white phosphorus was highly poisonous. Many workers became ill through contact with it, suffering from a disease nicknamed "phossy jaw." In Austria in 1845, Anton von Schrotter discovered red phosphorus. This was a much safer chemical that burst into flame only when rubbed against a special striking surface.

Matches quickly became part of everyday life. Modern safety matches usually have a mixture of chemicals in the heads and red phosphorus in the striking surface. "Strike anywhere" matches have a less poisonous form of phosphorus in the heads.

Prehistoric times	1600s	1805	1827	1833
People made fire by rubbing sticks together or striking stones together for sparks.	Flint and tinderboxes were used for lighting fires and lamps.	The first chemical-tipped matches were made in France.	John Walker starts selling his "safety" matches in his pharmacy.	The first match factories appear. Cheap matches are soon sold everywhere.

Electric Generator, 1831

Electricity had always been fascinating to scientists. In the 1600s, Otto von Guericke used **friction** to make spinning sulfur balls give off sparks. At parties, people were invited to touch them, and they jumped when they received a mild electric shock! Despite this, no one knew how to make, or generate, electricity so that it could be useful until the 1830s.

Making electricity

In 1752, Benjamin Franklin proved that lightning was a giant electric spark by the highly dangerous method of flying a kite in a thunderstorm. In 1800, Alessandro Volta of Italy made the first electric battery. For the first time, scientists were able to produce electric current long enough to experiment with this powerful force and find out more about it.

In 1820, the Danish scientist Hans Christian Oersted showed that an electric current would move a magnetized iron needle. A year later in Britain, Michael Faraday sat down with a Volta battery. He wanted to investigate the link between electricity and magnetism. Unknown to him, Joseph Henry in the United States was researching the subject at the same time. Both men reached the same conclusions about electricity and magnetism. They were the first to demonstrate **electromagnetic induction.**

Battersea Power Station in London was opened in 1935, burning coal to generate electricity for the city. Designed by a cathedral architect, it is no longer used as a power station, but its mighty chimneys stand as a monument to the old industrial age.

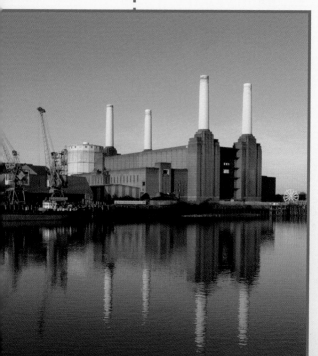

Faraday's experiment

Faraday passed a current from a battery through a wire suspended above a magnet. The wire rotated, which showed that the electric current was producing motion. He had shown how an electric motor might work. In 1831, Faraday showed that the process worked in reverse. When he rotated a copper disc through a magnetic field, he could produce an electric current and collect the current through metal wires touching the edge and center of the disc. He had made the first experimental generator.

The age of the dynamo

In 1832, French scientist Hippolyte Pixii made a working generator, using the Faraday principle. However, it took 40 years to develop generators big enough to deliver useful amounts of electric current. By the 1870s, electricity was poised to become the world's most useful energy source, replacing steam and gas in factories and in homes.

Galvani and the frogs' legs

In the 1780s, the Italian scientist Luigi Galvani was preparing an electrical experiment, skinning frogs' legs on a zinc metal plate. He was startled when the legs twitched! He decided that the frogs' legs must contain electricity. He got into an argument about this with Alessandro Volta, inventor of the battery. Galvani's frogs were "electric" because two metals, the zinc plate and the knife, were linked by a moist **conductor,** the frogs' legs. An electric current was produced by this **chemical reaction,** just as in Volta's battery. Galvani was not completely wrong—animals' bodies do contain a form of electricity in the nerve-muscle links.

How an electric generator works

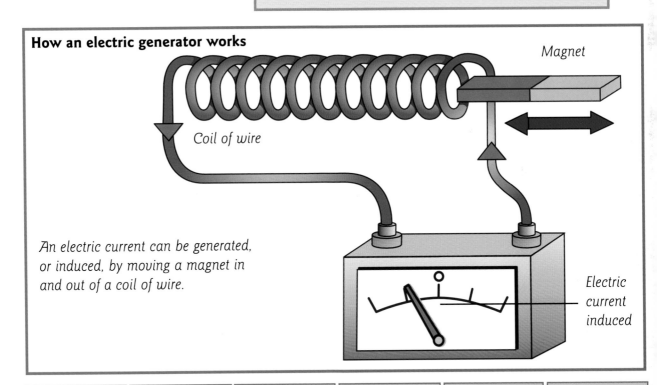

Magnet

Coil of wire

An electric current can be generated, or induced, by moving a magnet in and out of a coil of wire.

Electric current induced

1800	1820	1831	1850s	1879	1882
Alessandro Volta of Italy makes the first battery.	In Denmark, Hans Christian Oersted shows a wire carrying electric current is surrounded by a magnetic field.	Englishman Michael Faraday explains how electromagnetic induction can be used.	Small generators light arc lamps in theaters.	In the United States, Thomas Edison invents the electric light bulb.	New York City has the first power station that produces **direct current** (DC).

Mechanical Reaper, 1831

In 1800, farmers harvested their grain by hand, using sickles and **scythes,** in much the same way they had for the past 5,000 years. There had been some changes in farming during the 1700s, with some new machinery, such as seed drills, to boost food production. Farmers still did most jobs by hand, and a big farm needed many workers, especially at harvest time. The United States, in particular, was short of labor, and it was for the huge wheat fields that new grain cutting, or reaping, machines were invented.

The McCormick reaper

Cyrus McCormick grew up on a farm in Virginia. He watched his father try and fail to make a machine that would cut corn without ruining it, getting jammed, or harming its human operator. McCormick decided to try building one. In 1831, he made a machine that was a bit like a giant lawn mower, with a cutting blade that moved back and forth against a fixed guard and a bar to divide cut from uncut grain. A reel toppled the wheat stalks onto a platform, ready for tying. Between 1831 and 1840, he improved his reaper, testing it on wheat and oats, and began to sell it to other farmers. With a mechanical reaper, a farmer could harvest four times as much wheat per day than before.

In the nineteenth century, horse-drawn reapers did the harvesting. After being cut by the reaper, the corn would be raked into bundles.

Mechanical farming

Competition was fierce. There were lots of other new farm machines, including reapers. The first combine harvesters, which cut stalks and threshed the grain from the ears, appeared in the 1850s. McCormick's reaper succeeded because it was simple and reliable. Soon he moved his business to the fast-growing midwest city of Chicago, where his machines could be shipped to farms by boat and railroad.

As a combine harvester moves across a wheat field, it cuts the stalks of grain and removes the grain from the stalks by beating them. The grain drops through a grid, air blows off the outer shells, or husks, and the grain kernels are shot through a chute into a trailer.

McCormick continued to improve his reaper until it could do the work of ten men with scythes. In 1873, he introduced a reaper-binder, which tied up the cut wheat stalks into bales. Teams of up to 30 horses hauled whirling combine harvesters across the prairie wheat fields, and by the 1890s, gasoline-driven tractors began to replace horses. Farms got larger, yet fewer and fewer farmworkers were needed, a trend that continued right through the twentieth century.

Tull's drill

Jethro Tull, an English lawyer who became a farmer, invented the first mechanical seed sower, or seed drill, in 1701. For thousands of years, farmworkers had scattered seeds onto the soil, and many seeds were wasted. Tull's machine looked like a wheelbarrow. It planted seeds in neat rows, leaving space between the rows for weeding later. Like many inventors, Tull was ridiculed for his ideas, but he had the last laugh, living out his last years at his "Prosperous Farm."

100 C.E.	1831	1851	1854	1892	1908
Romans used a small hand-pushed harvester to cut wheat.	Cyrus McCormick invents his reaping machine.	Cyrus McCormick's reaper factory is claimed to be the world's biggest farm tool maker.	The first combine harvester goes to work in California.	In the United States, John Froelich invents the gasoline-powered tractor.	Motorized combine harvesters roll into action.

29

Electric Motor, 1834

There are electric motors all over modern houses, in CD players, in **vacuum** cleaners and washing machines, in electric shavers, in power tools, and in hair dryers. Electric motors power many of the machines we use every day.

Motors and generators

An electric motor turns electrical energy into mechanical energy or movement by using electricity, either from a battery or a generator. A generator turns mechanical energy into electrical energy. To nineteenth century scientists, this "reversal" was amazing.

In 1800, the electric motor was unknown. Scientists knew electricity existed, but they had little idea how to make it or use it. The breakthrough came when scientists realized that there was a connection between electricity and magnetism.

In 1820, Hans Christian Oersted of Denmark found that an electric current flowing near a compass needle caused the iron needle to move. André Marie Ampère turned this link into an important law of physics. Using this law, French inventor François Arago made the first **electromagnet** by passing an electric current through a coil of wire wrapped around a piece of iron.

Early electric motors, like this one which was made in 1839, used electro-magnetism to create electricity.

Which comes first: generator or motor?

Joseph Henry in the United States and Michael Faraday in Britain each came close to making an electric motor while trying to make an electric generator. They were exploring the new field of **electromagnetic induction.**
In 1834, a blacksmith from Vermont named Thomas Davenport used a battery to power the first working electric motor. He put it on a small railroad car, the first toy electric train.

Batteries produced very little power. In a world dominated by new steam engines, there was not much interest in electric motors. Until the 1880s, there were no big electrical generators, and no electricity supply to plug into. Even so, inventors such as Charles Grafton Page continued to work on electric motors. In 1873, a Belgian engineer named Zénobe Théophile Gramme demonstrated his new generator, or dynamo. To everyone's surprise, it worked just as well as an electric motor.

In the 1880s, the first power stations began supplying electricity to paying customers. At first they just wanted electric light, but they were soon eager to buy any electrical appliance. The motor to drive these things was now available, and so was the plug-in power supply.

Joseph Henry taught science at Princeton University and shares the honor with Michael Faraday of discovering electromagnetic induction. Henry once magnetized a needle using lightning 7.5 miles (12 km.) away!

AC and DC

The first electric motors used **alternating current** (AC). The **direct current** (DC) motor was invented in 1888 by Nikola Tesla. AC current reverses the direction of its flow about 50 times every second and is the kind of current available in most homes. DC current flows one way only and usually comes from a battery. Modern universal electric motors operate on either AC or DC electricity, switching the way they work depending on what source is available.

1820	1831	1834	1840	1873	1881
Frances Arago makes the first electromagnet.	Joseph Henry and Michael Faraday discover the principle of electrical induction.	In Vermont, Thomas Davenport builds the first toy electric train.	Alexander Bain makes the first electric clock.	Theophile Gramme's electric motor is the first that is big enough to be useful in machinery.	Nikola Tesla makes the first direct current (DC) electric motor.

Bunsen Burner, 1855

The Bunsen burner is a familiar piece of **apparatus** in a chemistry laboratory. It is a gas burner producing a flame that is controlled by opening and closing air holes around the base. A Bunsen burner is used to heat substances during an experiment.

Why heat matters

Fire was the first **chemical reaction** that people were able to make and control. People used fire to bake pottery and melt metals. Greek scientists realized more than 2,000 years ago that materials could have different states. For example, metal is a solid when cold, becomes a liquid when very hot, and then cools to a solid again.

The Bunsen gas burner has been used in science laboratories ever since 1855, when the humble burner was designed in its modern form.

In the 1700s, chemists began to understand more about what happens when substances are heated. The French scientist Antoine Lavoisier showed that burning was a chemical reaction, involving oxygen. In 1792, British engineer William Murdock lit his home using gas made by burning coal.

Bunsen and his burner

Robert Bunsen was a German chemistry professor. He made the Bunsen burner in 1855. Similar burners had been made earlier by Peter Desdega and Michael Faraday to help in their experiments. Bunsen's burner was better, because it burned coal gas without leaving a sooty deposit on the articles it heated. This made it useful in the laboratory and in the home. Burners working in the same way were used in gas lights, gas stoves, and gas fires. Multijet burners were used in furnaces to achieve very high temperatures.

A life of research

Robert Bunsen spent most of his working life as a professor at the University of Heidelberg in Germany. Experimenting with dangerous **chemicals** cost him the sight of one eye in an explosion, and he was nearly poisoned by arsenic. Bunsen was an inventor as well as a teacher. He studied **blast furnaces** to make steel-making more efficient. He invented an antidote to arsenic poisoning, a dry battery, a filter pump, and a device called a photometer for measuring light.

Bunsen's burner mixed air with gas before the gas was lit in proportions of three parts air to one part gas. By twisting a **valve** on the tube, the user could easily control the size and heat of the flame at the top. The burner proved so useful that its basic design has changed little in 150 years.

Analyzing light

Bunsen's chief interest was in light. With his colleague Gustav Kirchoff, he found that every **element** gives off light in a slightly different way when it is heated. By analyzing the light from different elements, they found that each one has its own light "signature."

1780s	1792	1855	1860	1861
Antoine Lavoisier shows that burning is a chemical reaction, a revolutionary step forward in chemistry.	British engineer William Murdock lights his home with coal gas, the first in the world.	Robert Bunsen designs burner to help in his experiments.	Robert Bunsen and Gustav Kirchoff discover a new element, cesium.	Robert Bunsen and Gustav Kirchoff discover a second new element, rubidium.

Cathode-ray Tube, 1879

Most people spend at least a few minutes, if not hours, every day looking at a **cathode-ray tube** of some kind. We use cathode-ray tubes to make images from electronic signals. Without cathode-ray tubes there would be no television, no computer screens or other visual display units, no radar sets or hospital oscilloscopes. The discovery of cathode rays, and their effects, had an enormous impact on the growth of modern electronics.

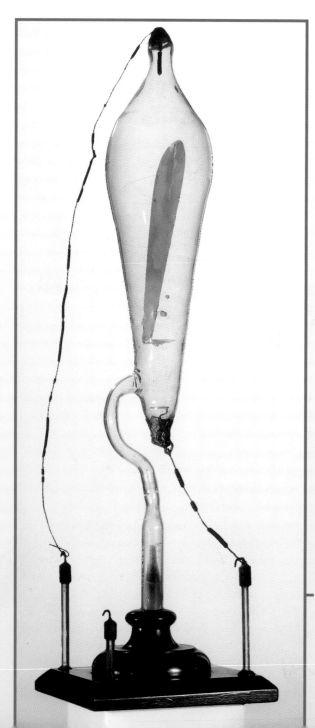

The tube that glowed

Cathode rays were unknown before the 1850s, when scientists began experimenting with electric currents passing along glass tubes filled with gases. Using an air pump to take out some of the air inside the tube, producing a **vacuum,** scientists noticed glowing colors inside the tube. Finally there was darkness, except at one end—the **anode** end, to which the electricity flowed. The glow was caused by cathode rays, a stream of high-speed **particles** coming from the cathode at the other end from which the electricity was flowing.

The inventor of the cathode-ray tube was Sir William Crookes. He was a British scientist who pioneered the study of cathode rays using glass vacuum tubes. These became known as Crookes tubes and produced cathode rays. Crookes discovered that the strange rays traveled in straight lines and produced light when they struck certain surfaces.

This vacuum tube was used by Crookes in about 1888 to investigate the deflection of cathode rays by a magnet.

Pictures in the tube

Scientists began using Crookes' cathode-ray tubes to explore the world of **radiation**. In Germany in 1895, Wilhelm Roentgen produced rays that showed the bones in his wife's hand. He called them X-rays. Two years later, the British scientist Joseph Thompson used a Crookes tube to discover **electrons.** Also in 1897, German radio researcher Ferdinand Braun was helping Guglielmo Marconi, the radio pioneer, when he invented a cathode-ray tube called the oscilloscope. Braun's tube was the starting point for many other exciting inventions.

These tubes would have a dramatic impact on the world of communications. First came the **diode** vacuum tube, invented by John Ambrose Fleming. In 1907 came the **triode,** invented by Lee De Forest. Without these two inventions, we might not have global telephones, radio, or television. The first television camera was made in 1931 by the Russian-born Vladimir Zworykin, working in the United States. The electronic television system, developed in the 1930s, triumphed over a rival mechanical scanning television system invented in the 1920s by John Logie Baird. The cathode-ray tube produced clearer pictures.

Radar, developed in the 1930s as "radiolocation," uses a cathode–ray tube display, similar to that in a television set or computer monitor. The **chemicals** on the inside of the screen glow when hit by a beam of electrons.

1858	1879	1897	1931	1936	1953
Julius Plucker of Germany studies gases inside glass tubes.	William Crookes announces his discovery of glowing energy inside vacuum tubes.	Ferdinand Braun invents the cathode-ray tube, or oscilloscope.	Russian Vladimir Zworkyin's iconoscope is the first television camera.	There are about 2,000 televisions in the world.	Color television is broadcast for the first time in the United States.

Steam Turbine, 1884

The steam engine dominated the nineteenth century on land and at sea. A more powerful engine, the steam **turbine,** which used very high-pressure steam to spin blades at great speed, opened up a new age of energy production. Today, turbines drive generators in electricity power stations, pump water for irrigation, power huge ships, and send jet planes roaring through the air.

How a turbine works

A turbine is basically a wheel turned by a force such as wind or water. The oldest turbines are waterwheels, which have been used for thousands of years. The windmill is another kind of turbine. The Ancient Greeks invented the steam turbine, but only as a toy. The principle of driving the blades of a fanlike wheel by air, water, or steam was understood. However, no one succeeded in making a steam turbine that was any better than manpower, horsepower, or wind power until the nineteenth century.

The turbine man

Charles Parsons, born into an important family, was a "modern" man who threw himself into the industrial world as a young engineer, working in northeast England. Steam turbines had been tried but always broke down because the power of the steam shattered the turbine blades. In 1884, Parsons designed a better turbine. He arranged the blades in rows, so that as the steam passed through in stages, much more steam energy was used but was better controlled. Parsons's engine did not spin itself to pieces.

Parsons installed four steam turbines in a power station in Newcastle, England, and then decided to try one in a ship.

Parsons fitted his steam turbine into a small launch, which he named Turbinia. *It is shown here cutting through the water, and its high speed convinced the Royal Navy that the turbine engine worked.*

His 44-ton (40-metric-ton) launch *Turbinia* startled the assembled crowds at the British naval review of 1897 as it dashed among the anchored battleships. It reached a speed of 34.5 knots (over 38 mph (62 kph), making it the fastest steamship of its day. The admirals who had scoffed at the idea were convinced, and turbines were soon being fitted to much bigger ships.

Modern turbines

Turbine technology continued to improve through the twentieth century. Huge, complex steam turbines drive cruise liners and large machines. The principle of the steam turbine led to the invention in the 1930s of the gas turbine engine, used in electricity generators, ships, a few very fast cars, and jet airplanes.

The Parsonses

Charles Parsons came from a family where everyone was enthusiastic about science. His father and his brother were astronomers. His father built the finest telescope of its time to study galaxies. Charles, a shy man, became well-known for his turbine boat but maintained the family interest in the stars. He founded the Grubb-Parsons company, which built many telescopes. He also invented a gramophone, mirrors for searchlights, and chains to keep car tires from skidding on the ice and snow.

How a steam turbine works

In a steam turbine, steam races through a series of wheels with blades. Fixed blades direct the steam onto moving blades around the shaft, which spins at high speeds.

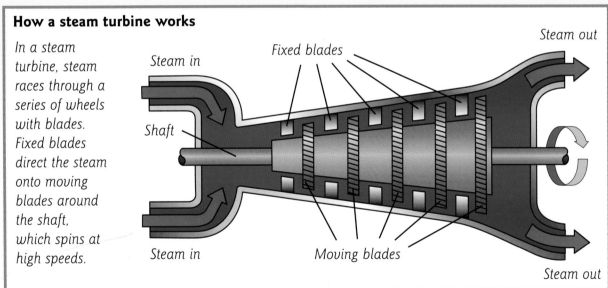

Steam in | Fixed blades | Steam out
Shaft
Steam in | Moving blades | Steam out

60 C.E.	1629	1791	1889	1896	1903	1930
Hero of Alexandria makes a steam turbine toy.	Giovanni Branca of Italy invents a steam turbine for use in a mill to stamp metal.	John Barber **patents** a simple gas turbine.	Charles Parsons builds his own steam turbines and electrical generators.	In the United States, Charles G. Curtis invents a multi-stage steam turbine.	Armengaud and Lemale in France build the first modern gas turbine.	Frank Whittle invents the first turbojet engine for aircraft.

Internal Combustion
Engine, 1885

Can a steam engine work without steam? This idea attracted inventors in the mid-1800s. Steam engines were big, dirty, expensive, and sometimes dangerous. There was a market for smaller, cheaper engines to drive light machinery, and steam cars on the roads had been unsuccessful. The answer could be an **internal combustion engine.** Instead of having a fire and boiler, like a steam engine, this new engine would be driven by explosions of burning fuel inside **cylinders.**

By the 1890s, more and more cars with internal combustion engines were appearing on the roads. There were also steam and electric cars, but the gasoline engine won in the end.

The dash for gas

What fuel could be used? As early as 1794, inventors experimented with engines burning various fuels, including dangerous mixtures of turpentine and air. Fuel was a problem. Today, we take petroleum for granted, but before 1850 very little petroleum oil was available. There were hardly any oil wells. Coal gas made from burning coal in "gasworks" was available in many big towns, however.

Putting the engine on wheels

In 1877, German engineer Nikolaus Otto **patented** a coal gas engine that worked on the same "four-stroke" principle as modern car engines. Unfortunately, it was not good for cars because it was a fixed engine, burning gas piped into it from local gasworks.

Otto's friend, Gottfried Daimler, went to work on the problem. Unknown to him, so did another German, Karl Benz. Benz made and sold his own gas engines to raise money for work on his dream, a "horseless carriage" driven by an engine burning a mixture of gasoline and air. He was helped by his wife Berta. They faced the challenging task of designing a new vehicle and engine, adapting existing steam and coal gas engine technology where possible.

The automobile revolution

Berta Benz watched Karl drive their first three-wheeled car in 1885. Later that year, Daimler also showed off a three-wheeled motor vehicle, though Benz's was more like the car we know today. In 1888, Berta Benz took her two sons on the first long cross-country car ride, to a neighboring town. She bought fuel from a pharmacy, the only kind of shop that sold gasoline.

The **internal combustion engine** revolutionized transportation. It changed the way people worked and the look of the landscape. Cars needed roads, and roads changed many towns and cities, not always for the better. Cars needed fuel, too, and a huge new industry came into being—the oil industry. The car engine brought many benefits and also many problems, such as congestion and pollution, which scientists and environmentalists in the twenty-first century have to solve.

1794	1826	1860	1876	1885	1897
Robert Street invents a **piston** pump driven by an exploding mixture of turpentine and air.	Samual Brown of Britain tests a hydrogen gas engine in a carriage but abandons the idea.	Etienne Lenoir of France builds the first coal gas engine.	Nikolaus Otto builds the first efficient four-stroke engine.	In Germany, Karl Benz and Gottfried Daimler take to the road in their motor vehicles.	Rudolf Diesel invents the diesel engine.

Bakelite, 1909

In 1909 Leo Baekeland, a Belgian scientist working in the United States, **patented** a way to make "the material of a thousand uses." He called it bakelite and it was a kind of plastic. Plastics can be made in almost any shape or color and can be soft or hard. Before plastics, people had only natural materials such as bone, ivory, horn, and leather. They sat on wooden chairs, wore woolen or cotton clothing, and drank from pottery or metal cups.

Bakelite was not the first plastic. In 1862, Alexander Parkes, a British chemist, invented a shell-like plastic he called parkesine. It was used for combs and cutlery handles. In 1870, the Hyatt brothers in the United States produced another plastic called celluloid, to replace natural ivory in billiard balls. It was also used for false teeth and piano keys. Unfortunately, it went soft when heated.

This Bakelite radio became a fashion item in the early twentieth century. It is an example of a new technology (radio) making use of new materials (plastics). People liked plastics because they gave their homes a modern look.

How bakelite changed the world

Bakelite was the first useful plastic and sold widely. Baekeland first tried to make **synthetic** rubber, using two common organic **chemicals,** formaldehyde and phenol. Instead, he produced a hard resin that could be shaped when heated but then stayed hard and would not melt. It could be dyed in many colors. It held water and it was an **insulator.** Soon, manufacturers were making bakelite doorknobs, telephones, and radio cabinets. It was used for records, too.

In 1922, German chemist Hermann Staudinger revealed the secret of plastics. They were made of polymers, long chains of thousands of **molecules,** linked together to create one

The nylon revolution

In 1935, Wallace H. Carothers, a researcher working for DuPont in the United States, invented the first synthetic fiber, nylon, which went on sale in 1938. Unfortunately, he missed the success of the new material, for he took his own life in an episode of depression in 1937. Nylon was used to make women's stockings (replacing more expensive silk stockings), toothbrush bristles, and during World War II it was used for parachute cords.

giant molecule. Cotton is made from a natural polymer, cellulose. The 1930s brought fast developments in plastics, with the first commercial use of four important new materials—acrylic, nylon, polystyrene, and polyvinyl chloride (PVC).

We live in a plastic world

The plastic revolution really sped up in the 1950s, and it has had a huge impact on everyday life. In fact, there are plastics everywhere you look! The trouble with plastics is that they last too long. Getting rid of them can be a problem because a plastic bag or bottle, once thrown away, will still be there in a hundred years. Scientists have the challenge of finding better ways of recycling plastics and inventing more biodegradable plastics that will not pollute the environment.

Too much plastic waste is either buried or burned. It makes more sense to recycle as many plastic bottles and containers as possible. Some plastics can be melted down and reformed, while others are powdered for use as filling material.

1870	1909	1935	1938	1965	1989
John W. Hyatt and Isaiah Hyatt invent celluloid.	In the United States, Leo Baekeland **patents** bakelite.	Wallace H. Carothers, working for DuPont, invents nylon.	Roy J. Plunkett invents Teflon later used in non-stick pans.	In the U.S., Stephanie Kwolek invents kevlar, a plastic fiber tough enough to stop a bullet.	Biodegradable plastics appear. They break down naturally after they are thrown away.

Nuclear Power, 1945

Many discoveries and inventions led to one of the key moments in science, the day in July 1945 when the first atomic bomb was exploded in the New Mexico desert. This was the start of the nuclear age. The scientists who invented this most terrible of weapons also hoped to give the world a source of limitless energy.

In the 1950s, many people believed that nuclear power would replace burning coal and oil for making electricity. Unfortunately, the dream of limitless cheap, clean energy has not yet been realized.

Background to the breakthrough

Ever since 1911, when Ernest Rutherford proved that the **atom** had a **nucleus,** a new breed of scientists called nuclear physicists had been unraveling the secrets of the atom. They had discovered tiny **particles,** such as the neutron. They had shown that an **element** could be made during a **chain reaction** by bombarding another element with neutrons. This was done in 1938 by two German researchers, Otto Hahn and Fritz Strassmann, who made barium by splitting uranium atoms. The following year, the Austrian scientist Lise Meitner explained what had happened. Hahn and Strassmann had created a nuclear **fission** chain reaction that had produced more energy than it used up.

War and the new power

The immense power released in this way had awesome possibilities. The incredible energy of a chain reaction had been predicted in 1905 by the brilliant German scientist Albert Einstein. Using Einstein's ideas, scientists calculated that splitting a tiny piece of uranium would release as much energy as thousands of tons of explosive. By 1939, the world was at war. Einstein warned the Allies that Nazi Germany might build an atomic bomb.

At once, a team of scientists began to work at the University of Chicago. Led by an Italian-born physicist named Enrico Fermi, they built a test reactor in a room under the college football field. There, on December 2, 1942, they set off, and stopped, the first controlled chain reaction. They had proved that atomic power was possible.

The nuclear age

The world was startled when two atomic bombs were dropped on Japan in 1945. This brought World War II to an end. After the war, both the U.S. and Soviet governments began developing even more destructive weapons. The first nuclear power stations were opened in the United States in 1957. The heat from nuclear reactions was used to drive steam turbines to generate electricity. Scientists promised cheap power forever.

Unfortunately, nuclear power turned out to be more expensive than had been thought, as well as more dangerous. Accidents such as those at Three Mile Island in Pennsylvania in 1979, and at Chernobyl in the former USSR in 1986, made people fearful of the deadly polluting **radiation** that nuclear power can create. Nuclear energy could meet all the world's energy needs, but only if science can solve the safety and waste disposal problems.

The Japanese city of Hiroshima was destroyed by the atomic bomb dropped on August 6, 1945, and 75,000 people were killed. This was the first awesome demonstration of nuclear power.

1942	1945	1952	1954	1957	1986
In Chicago, Enrico Fermi's team achieve the first controlled nuclear reaction.	The first atomic bombs destroy the Japanese cities of Hiroshima and Nagasaki.	The United States tests the first hydrogen bomb, more powerful than any atomic bomb.	The U.S. submarine *Nautilus* is the first nuclear powered vessel.	The first large-scale nuclear power plant in the world begins operations in Shippingsport, Pennsylvania.	An accident at the Chernobyl power station in the former Soviet Union causes fears about nuclear power.

Timeline

60 C.E.	Hero of Alexandria makes a steam turbine toy.
900	The Chinese discover how to make gunpowder.
850	Porcelain is invented in China.
1100s	The Chinese discover the magnifying power of a **lens.**
1590	Zacharias Jansen makes first microscope.
1592	Galileo Galilei makes first working thermometer.
1608	The telescope is invented.
1643	Evangelista Torricelli makes first **mercury**-filled barometer.
1650	Otto von Guericke invents the air pump.
1707	Porcelain is first made in Europe by Johann Bottger.
1712	Thomas Newcomen designs the first practical steam engine.
1733	John Kay invents the flying shuttle, which speeds up **weaving.**
1759	John Harrison builds his H4 watch, the first practical chronometer.
1792	William Murdock's home becomes the first in the world to be heated by coal gas.
1793	Eli Whitney's cotton gin does the work of 50 people on plantations in the United States.
1800	Alessandro Volta of Italy makes the first battery.
1804	Richard Trevithick builds the first successful steam carriage.
1805	The first **chemical**-tipped matches are made in France.
1820	François Arago makes first **electromagnet.**
1827	John Walker starts selling his safety matches in his pharmacy.

1831	Michael Faraday explains how **electromagnetic induction** can be used to make an electricity generator.
	Cyrus McCormick invents his reaper.
1834	Thomas Davenport makes the first working electric motor.
1854	The first combine harvester goes to work in California.
1855	Robert Bunsen designs a burner to help in his experiments.
1866	Alfred Nobel of Sweden invents dynamite.
1876	Nikolaus Otto builds the first efficient four-stroke engine.
1879	William Crookes invents the **cathode-ray tube.**
1884	Charles Parsons invents the steam **turbine.**
1885	Karl Benz and Gottfried Daimler separately invent the **internal combustion engine.**
1892	Sir James Dewar invents the **vacuum** bottle, first used to keep liquids cool in the laboratory.
1909	Leo Baekeland **patents** bakelite, the first **synthetic** plastic.
1931	Vladimir Zworykin's iconoscope is the first television camera.
1942	Enrico Fermi's team produce the first controlled nuclear **chain reaction.**
1945	The first atomic bombs destroy the Japanese cities of Hiroshima and Nagasaki.
1965	The first astronaut leaves a spacecraft through an air lock.
1989	Biodegradable plastics are introduced. They break down naturally after they are thrown away.
1995	The Navstar navigation system can pinpoint a ship's position using **satellite** data.

Glossary

acid chemical substance that produces hydrogen when dissolved in water

alternating current electric current that flows back and forth

anode positive electrode in an electrical circuit

apparatus equipment such as bottles, tubes, and electrical circuits used in scientific experiments

atom smallest part of an element that can take part in a chemical reaction

bearings metal balls or rollers used to ease moving parts and reduce friction

bimetallic strip two strips of different metals fastened together. One heats up more quickly than the other, causing the strip to bend.

blast furnace very hot oven for making iron and steel

cathode-ray tube vacuum tube in which a beam of electrons is projected onto a fluorescent screen

cell smallest unit of a living thing

ceramic substance made from clay heated in a kiln until hard, such as a tile, brick, or pot

chain reaction process that goes on repeating itself once its started

chemical substance such as a gas, liquid, or solid used in chemistry

chemical reaction process of change that begins when two substances come into contact and affect one another, sometimes producing a new substance

concave curved like the inside of a bowl

condense to change from gas into a liquid. If steam or water vapor hits a cool surface, it condenses into droplets of water.

conductor material through which heat or electricity moves easily

convex curved like the outside of a bowl

Crusader Christian soldier in the holy wars in the Middle Ages

cylinder long, round chamber into which a piston fits

dense heavy, containing more matter

diode electronic part that allows electric current to flow only in one direction

direct current electric current that flows in one direction

electromagnet kind of magnet that uses electricity. Electromagnetism is the force produced when an electric current flows through a coil of wire.

electromagnetic induction using an electric current and a magnet to produce motion, or using motion and a magnet to produce an electric current

electron tiny particle inside an atom that carries a negative electrical charge

element substance made up of atoms that are all alike. An element cannot be separated into simpler parts.

fission the splitting of the nuclei of atoms releasing enormous energy. Fission occurs in a nuclear reaction.

friar Christian holy man who lives a simple life of teaching and prayer

friction force that tries to keep one surface from sliding against another

Industrial Revolution social, economic, and scientific changes that began in Western Europe in the 1700s, leading to the growth of factories and the use of machines

inflammable able to burn easily

insulator material that does not conduct electricity or heat

internal combustion engine device that uses a fuel such as burning gas mixed with air to power a machine

latitude distance of a place north or south of the equator

lens curved piece of glass or other transparent material that lets light through it, either bringing together or spreading the rays

longitude distance of a place east or west of a line linking the North and South poles

mercury silvery metal that is liquid at room temperature

molecule the smallest part into which a substance can be cut without being changed chemically into a different substance

nucleus center of an atom

particle very tiny piece of something. Atomic particles are the parts that make up an atom.

patent official document confirming ownership of a particular invention or process

piston rod with a wide end that moves up and down inside a pump or the cylinder of a car engine

prodigy someone with remarkable talent, especially when young

radiation energy given off in the form of light, electricity, or heat

satellite small body moving around a larger one, held in its path or orbit by the force of gravity of the larger body

scythe tool with a curving blade attached to a long handle

slave someone who is forced to work without pay

spinning twisting strands of wool or cotton together to make thread or yarn

synthetic artificially made

textile any material made by weaving fabrics, such as cloth or carpets

triode electronic device called a vacuum tube with three parts or electrodes

vacuum space with little or no air in it, where pressure is much less than normal atmospheric pressure

valve device for opening and closing, to allow something like blood, steam, air, or electric current to flow

weaving technique used to make textiles by criss-crossing threads on a machine called a loom

More Books to Read

Casanellas, Antonio. *Great Discoveries and Inventions*. Milwaukee: Gareth Stevens Inc., 2000.

Erlbach, Arlene. *The Kids' Invention Book*. Minneapolis: The Lerner Publishing Group, 1998.

Sachs, Jessica Snyder. *The Encyclopedia of Inventions*. Danbury, Conn.: Franklin Watts Inc., 2001.

Index